Life's Lessons from Mayberry

Life's Lessons from Mayberry

by

Len and John Oszustowicz

THE SUMMIT PUBLISHING GROUP
Arlington, Texas

THE SUMMIT PUBLISHING GROUP
One Arlington Centre, 1112 East Copeland Road, Fifth Floor
Arlington, Texas 76011
summit@dfw.net
www.summitbooks.com

Printed in the United States of America.

01 00 99 98 97   010   5 4 3 2 1

Library of Congress Cataloging-in-Publication Data
Oszustowicz, Len.
    Life's lessons from Mayberry : a book of wisdom and wit from
        America's favorite small town / by Len and John Oszustowicz.
        p. cm.
    ISBN 1-56530-250-8
        1. Andy Griffith show (Television program) I. Oszustowicz, John.
        II. Title.
PN1992.77.A573092 1997   97-4918
791.45'72--dc21   cip

Cover design by Davidson Design
Book design by Michael Melton

The authors wish to acknowledge the following references:

Richard Kelly, *The Andy Griffith Show*. Winston-Salem, NC: John F. Blair, Publisher, 1981.

Ken Beck and Jim Clark, *The Andy Griffith Show Book*. New York: St. Martin's Press, 1985.

Introduction

The mythical North Carolina town of Mayberry has added as much to the fabric of American culture as nearly any other community in the country—real or imagined. For nearly four decades, the picture of its people sharing the richness of life together in a peaceful setting has set the standard for the best that American life has to offer. *Life's Lessons from Mayberry* captures the message of Mayberry and offers it in a down-home style as warm and relaxed as Andy's front porch.

These homespun bits of Mayberry wisdom have been gathered from episodes of *The Andy Griffith Show,* each one referring to a scene from the show where that message was featured. For those who are not familiar with the show, this reference serves as an illustration. For devoted Mayberry fans, these references will conjure a hundred images of the original show and will also bring to mind many other scenes from this timeless piece of television history. In either case, the point of *Life's Lessons from Mayberry* is to remind us of the lessons we can all learn from the lives of the good citizens of Mayberry, America's favorite small town.

The prettiest things are sometimes wrapped in burlap.

Andy and Ellie saw the beauty of a "plain" farm girl—and changed her life.

People who mind their own business shouldn't be considered odd by those who don't.

Barney thought Sam, a quiet farmer, was a crook. Come to find out, he was a gentle, private man who handled his life's business in his own way.

Look for the worm before you bite into the apple.

When Barney went looking for a new car, he got so starry-eyed over his treasure that he forgot to check out the story of "Hubcaps" Lesch, who ran a used-car scam out of Raleigh. Ol' Barn paid dearly for his mistake.

The dream is sometimes better than the real thing.

For years, Floyd dreamed of having a two-chair barbershop. When he finally got one, he couldn't wait to get back to worrying about just one head at a time.

Clover sometimes grows over the briar patch.

The Morrison sisters, "innocent" old ladies, got caught operating a still in Mayberry. The long arm of the Mayberry P.D. shut them down with Otis as the prime informant.

The more time a parent spends with a child, the better both of their lives will be.

Aunt Bee thought Opie spent too much time at the jailhouse—she forgot that Andy was at the jailhouse, too.

Always take the high road; the view's better.

Andy caught old Luke stealing cows. Andy never once said "I told you so" to Mayor Stoner or the state inspector who made fun of Andy's common-sense approach.

Buy quality . . . it's cheaper in the long run.

Barney's old salt-and-pepper suit lasted long and looked great year after year—and always hung just right in "the dips."

Andy: Well? [Why aren't you leaving with the detective from Raleigh?]

Barney: I just . . . uh . . . thought I'd . . . uh . . . wait with you a spell.

Andy: Well, I appreciate that, Barn. But the mayor could be right. It [my way to catch the cow thief] could be kind of a hare-brained idea.

Barney: Well, I'll take my chances. I was almost out to the car, and I got to remembering another time a few years back when another mayor of our town accused you of having a hare-brained idea. Remember that? That was when you had the idea of makin' me your deputy.

From: "The Cow Thief"
Original Air Date: October 29, 1962

The "F" in fun stands for friends.

Barney and Thelma Lou were a happy pair—all they needed was a pan of cashew fudge and a George Raft movie.

No amount of money is worth a good night's sleep.

Aunt Bee saved money on her meat order but was bothered by her conscience when she chose not to deal with her regular butcher, Mr. Foley.

Be careful when playing the peacemaker…you might get caught in the crossfire.

Andy learned real fast that there is no neutral ground on the battlefield of love. Neither Thelma Lou nor Barney appreciated him stickin' his nose where it didn't belong.

Aunt Bee: Mr. Foley, could I ask a tremendous favor of you?

Mr. Foley: Why sure, Aunt Bee, what is it?

Aunt Bee: I have this friend, and she bought all this beef—a whole side of it. She didn't buy it from you; she wishes now that she had. Her freezer's broken now, and I was wondering—I mean, she was wondering—if you could store it for her.

Mr. Foley: Sure, Miss Bee, you just tell your friend to bring it over, and I'll be glad to store it for her.

Aunt Bee: I know it's asking a lot, but you don't know how terribly grateful I will—I mean, my friend—will be. And she'll be willing to pay for it.

Mr. Foley: Nonsense. You've been too good a customer for too long. You tell your friend that any friend of yours is a friend of mine.

From: "Bargain Day"
Original Air Date: March 23, 1964

Expect others to do their best, not yours.

Andy allowed Barney to handle a tough arrest although Andy would have done it differently— and it worked out just fine.

Education isn't the same as wisdom.

Time and again, mountain man Briscoe Darling came down from the hills and proved to Andy that experience and common sense are just as important as "book learning."

If you can't be part of the
solution, stay out of the problem
so you don't add to it.

Andy tried to speed up Barney's courting of
Thelma Lou; his interference did more harm
than good. Things only got better when Andy
minded his own business.

Remember where you came from
...you may need to go back.

Guitar player Jim Lindsey thought he had out-grown his hometown. When times got tough, Mayberry was what he needed most.

Andy: There's something wrong with Opie.

Hobo: I hope nothing serious; I've grown fond of that boy. What's wrong?

Andy: There seems to be something wrong with his thinkin'. He's a little twisted on things lately, like being able to tell the difference between right and wrong. Not that that's an easy thing. Lots of grown-ups still strugglin' with that same problem. But it's extra difficult for a youngster, 'cause things rub off on 'em so easy. You can't let a young 'un decide for himself; he'll grab at the first flashy thing with a fancy ribbon on it. When he finds out there's a hook in it, it's too late. Wrong ideas come packaged with so much fancy glitter that it's not easy to convince him that other things might be better in the long run. All a parent can do is say wait, trust me, and to try to keep temptation away.

From: "Opie's Hobo Friend"
Original Air Date: November 13, 1961

Sometimes concern comes wrapped in "unkind" packages.

Druggist Ellie Walker got off on the wrong foot in Mayberry when she wouldn't give hypochondriac Emma Watson the medicine she didn't need.

Don't open old wounds.

Time had healed an old wound between two of Mayberry's finest citizens, Floyd and Charlie Foley...until Barney reopened the case.

The line between salesmanship and untruth is often as thin as a whisker.

Opie and Barney believed that Andy's sales tactics crossed the line when Andy sold the town's "historic" cannon.

Dignity is more valuable than gold.

Aunt Bee mistakenly believed that she was no longer important to Andy and Opie, but of course, she was forever a part of the Taylor family.

Common sense endures.

Andy's solution for catching an escaped convict with his leaky rowboat, although not fancy or "big city," was very effective.

Playing games with another's heart is a dangerous business.

Barney's occasional attempts to make Thelma Lou jealous always backfired and left him begging her forgiveness.

Base your opinion on the facts— not vice versa.

Andy assumed that Helen planned to marry Mayberry's handsome new doctor and learned that jumping to conclusions is bad business, especially when you underestimate those who are closest to you.

Words are tools: Truth is a shovel to uncover; gossip is a knife to cut.

The men of Mayberry thought that a salesman was really a talent scout; a lot of fine citizens came away with bruised egos (not to mention unneeded shoes).

Give children a chance . . . they'll teach grown-ups a lot about character.

When Opie found a wallet full of money, he gave it back to its owner; Andy, once again, had underestimated the boy.

Barney: But Andy, what [Opie] told you is impossible.

Andy: Well, a whole lot of times, I've asked him to believe things that to his mind must have seemed just as impossible.

Barney: Oh, but Andy, this silver hat and the jingling and the smoke from the ears—what about all that?

Andy: Oh, I don't know, Barn. I guess it's a time like this when you're asked to believe something that just don't seem possible. That's the moment that decides whether you got faith in somebody or not.

Barney: But how can you explain it all?

Andy: I can't.

Barney: But you do believe in Mr. McBeevee?

Andy: No, but I believe in Opie.

From: "Mr. McBeevee"
Original Air Date: October 1, 1962

Truth and discretion must be gently balanced.

Opie's journalism career was short-lived when he printed the truth, the whole truth, and nothing but the truth, and his reporting of "adult" conversations about citizens caused an uproar in Mayberry.

A child's heart is more fragile than glass and more resilient than a basketball.

When Opie fell for Miss Crump, he got a first-hand lesson on both the pain and the joy of "puppy" love. Helen broke his heart, but Opie made a quick recovery.

Be proud of your heritage.

Otis, the town tippler, was found to be a descendant of a Revolutionary War hero. Otis stood taller as a result.

Rejoice in the success of others.

Andy and Barney had more confidence in Rafe Hollister's musical ability than he had in himself. When he sang for Founders Day, he felt good, and they felt better.

Andy: What you saving this old rock for? Is it worth anything?

Barney: Well, not money-wise, but it has a lot of sentimental value. It was my daddy's rock.

Andy: Oh, I'm sorry, Barn.

Barney: Oh, listen. Don't feel sad. There's a lot of happiness connected with that rock.

Andy: There is?

Barney: Yeah. It used to sit on my daddy's desk. I used to strike kitchen matches on it and hold them to my daddy's pipe. You know, for a little fella, it was a big kick to strike a match and hold it to your dad's pipe.

From: "Class Reunion"
Original Air Date: February 4, 1963

Overestimating yourself is the quickest road to humility.

Andy thought he was the cat's meow, but he soon learned otherwise when he was outdone at the shooting range...by a woman.

Sometimes the medicine is worse than the disease.

Opie's arithmetic troubles caused Andy to over-react. What was a relatively minor problem (that "Ope" ended up solving for himself) threw everything into an uproar.

Common sense is more reliable than a well-oiled clock.

Mayberry's police department was accused of being behind the times. All it did was keep the peace and catch bad guys.

Even well-intentioned lies get us into trouble.

Aunt Bee invented a boyfriend for herself to try to spare Andy his concern for her loneliness, and she nearly hurt many innocent people in the process.

Friendship sometimes calls for tough decisions…choose wisely.

Opie learned that keeping a runaway friend's secret required him to choose between obedience and trust.

Sometimes we hurt our friends most when we try to be funny.

Townsfolk made fun of Barney when he arrested them for minor violations. They didn't understand his sincerity.

Sometimes "money problems" come from having too much.

Rich landlord Ben Weaver threatened to put a family out of their home when they couldn't pay their small rent. Instead, he learned compassion when his heart was warmed by the spirit of Christmas.

Often "I can if I think I can," even if I can't.

Andy convinced "loser" Edgar Bennett that he was a "winner." All it took was a warm smile and a kind word—and it didn't cost a dime.

Trust, though sometimes painful, is always rewarded.

Andy had to convince Opie that their new housekeeper, Aunt Bee, would be a blessing to the sheriff and his son.

Jump to conclusions, then be ready for the long fall.

When Andy found out that Ellie could get on just fine without him, he mended his ways.

Talent is good. Luck ain't bad, either.

The crook that Barney captured promised to even the score. Thank goodness Andy was around to help chase the villain down the second time.

Walk quietly and with dignity. Talking is the easy part; good deeds aren't so easy.

Andy's quiet, calm style was usually the best way to solve a sheriffin' problem. He proved that when he set up a crook by using Emma Brand's apple pie as bait.

If you refuse an offer of help, do it graciously. You might want to reconsider down the road.

The "state boys" and the "feds" often found out that they should respect an offer of help from the Mayberry P.D.

Keep your nose out of other folks' business—especially the business of the heart.

Andy learned a good lesson when he tried to play peacemaker between Barney and Thelma Lou. Although his heart was in the right place, his meddling almost caused a permanent split-up.

Sometimes the hardest role to play is yourself.

Mayberry townsfolk abandoned their simple ways trying to impress a movie producer—and made fools of themselves in the bargain.

Praise is better heard than spoken.

Jim Lindsey, a homegrown guitar player, misled townspeople about his success—and was trimmed down to size when he had to own up to the truth.

Trust your loved ones...tell them when they do something out of character.

Opie appeared lazy when he let another boy beat him out of a job at the market—until Andy learned that the other boy needed the money to help feed his family. Floyd said Opie was a "prince" for giving up the job.

Andy: You sound like you meant to get fired. Now I want you to tell me why you got fired, and I want you to tell me the truth.

Opie: You see, this other boy, Billy, he wanted the job to pay some bills. His Paw's been sick...well, they've got some bills.

Andy: I'm sorry.

Opie: That's OK.

Andy: You know when I was bragging on you to Floyd and Goober? I told 'em how proud I was to have a boy like you. But that's not quite true. You're a man.

From: "Opie's Job"
Original Air Date: September 13, 1965

It doesn't take much to boost the confidence of a friend who's down.

When Ernest T. Bass came down from the mountains looking for respect, all it took was one of Barney's old whipcord uniforms to give him back his self-confidence. After that, he was his old, ornery, cantankerous self again.

Jealousy short-circuits the brain.

Helen's teacher friend made Andy jealous and turned his brain to mush...she caused him to do foolish things he never would have done if he was thinking straight.

Understand the sensitivities of children.

Opie's world was turned upside down when his beloved Rose departed for marriage and the gentle, but unknown, Aunt Bee arrived.

Accept people as you find them ...the more you try to change a person, the more miserable you'll both be.

For all of his good intentions, Andy shouldn't have tried to make a Boston gentleman out of Ernest T. Bass—after all, "Romeena" fell for the real Ernest T., not the suave socialite.

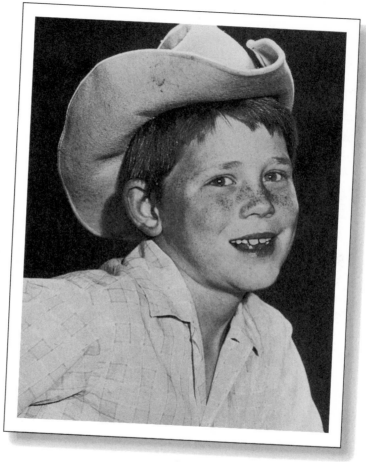

Do your best work, then stand by it.

Barney worried that he would be replaced by an upstart lawman. He later found that his best was good enough for Andy. Barney's big heart and ready smile more than made up for his lack of fancy lawman tactics.

You've got to look through the brush to find a raspberry…it's the hidden virtue that counts.

When Ellie ran for town council, she found that in Mayberry the best "man" for the job couldn't be a woman. In the end, Ellie's goodness, wisdom and charm changed all that.

In tough times, rally around family.

Even though cousin Virgil was clumsy and almost wrecked the courthouse, Barney never gave up on him.

When you're right, don't back down.

Opie had to face up to a bully and found out that it's more important to be tough on the inside than on the outside. Bruised arms and legs heal a lot faster than bruised self-respect.

Don't spread rumors…they hurt people even when they're not supposed to.

Barney's well-meaning "scoop" that Helen and Andy were getting married didn't do any real harm, but it did cause a lot of confusion.

Pride is like crystal: easy to break and hard to fix.

Ernest T. Bass was a crossing guard—uniform and all. When he was replaced by Malcolm Merriweather, he was cut deeply.

Wisdom is earned through experiences, good and bad.

Opie learned that misplaced loyalty can do more harm than good. When he protected Tex, his runaway friend, he learned that his Paw is not only older, but wiser.

Don't tamper with the emotions of others. It's a quick path to heartache.

Thelma Lou didn't want Barney to get too sure of himself in their courtin', so she tried to use Gomer to show him who was the boss. The whole thing almost went "blooey."

Be careful when you do your thinkin' with your heart.

Floyd and Barney were deceived by a wily female speeder, who played to her strength and the boys' weakness.

Be careful of people who flatter you.

When Barney got involved with a new girl who tried to drag him to the altar, he learned that it's hard not to believe people when they say nice things about you.

Houseguests are like the garbage.
Both need to be out of the house
after a few days.

The Taylors took Gomer in to nurse his sore back. Before long, Gomer's hurt back became Andy's pain in the neck.

Sharing a treasure means more than keeping it to yourself.

When Howard caught "Old Sam" out of Tucker's Lake, he was a Mayberry celebrity. He learned that the real way to share with his friends was to release the silver carp and not to put him in the famous fish display at the Raleigh Aquarium.

Have fun, but use your head.

Even Aunt Bee got carried away having fun with the "snake oil" salesman. Fortunately, it didn't take her long to regain her footing.

One's misery is another's happiness.

A Mayberry couple were only "happy" when they were at each other's throats. It worked that way for nearly fifty years.

Sometimes even Mother Nature needs a little help.

The whole Taylor household had to give nature a hand to help Barney pass his physical. It was worth it to keep Bernard P. Fife, M.D. (Mayberry Deputy) on the job.

A bad wig is worse than no hair at all.

Mr. Schwump, perennial wallflower, might have been a real man about town—except for that hairpiece.

Even the rules leave room for common sense.

Deputy Warren applied the rules to the letter and forgot that rules are made for people.

Look for talent in people, not places.

A record producer found that there is musical talent everywhere—even in small-town America.

If you break something...fix it.

When Opie killed a mother robin, Andy helped him understand the importance of responsibility by reminding him that the baby birds still had to be cared for.

Look for beauty in the soul; it is ageless.

Andy saw true beauty in the heart of a kind lady who devoted herself to making the Founders Day pageant a success.

When good fortune comes your way, shut up and enjoy it.

Aunt Bee won prizes but lost friends when she rattled on to her neighbors about her good fortune.

Protect the feelings of your friends—at almost any cost.

Aunt Bee could make almost anything—except pickles. But rather than hurt her feelings, Andy, Barney, and Opie ate gallons of her "kerosene cucumbers."

Slow down...enjoy life.

Dr. Breen of New York City helped even the gentle people of Mayberry remember to stop and enjoy the beauty of their little town.

Listen to both sides...then make up your mind.

Andy was the town's greatest judge of everything from singing to pickles, and he proved time and again that the scales of justice were well-balanced in Mayberry.

Barney: You know what I think I'm gonna do?

Mr. Tucker: What?

Barney: I'm going to go home and have a little nap, then go over to Thelma Lou's and watch a little TV. Yeah, I believe that's what I'll do. Go home, have a nap. Then over to Thelma Lou's for TV. Um. Yep, that's the plan. Go home, have a little nap…

Mr. Tucker: For the love of Mike, do it. Do it. Just do it. Take a nap. Go to Thelma Lou's for TV.

Barney: What's the hurry?

From: "Man in a Hurry"
Original Air Date: January 14, 1963

A person doesn't necessarily need to be efficient to be effective.

When Wally fired Gomer for doodling on the job at the filling station, he realized that it was Gomer's humor and friendliness that made the business a success, not his efficiency.

Don't judge another's charity. . . you don't know what's in their heart.

Andy thought that Opie was being selfish until he found out that he was saving for something very special. As it turned out, Opie's gift was the most generous of all.

Overlook differences…focus on similarities.

When Helen Crump's niece came into town, Opie was determined to show her up—until he found out that she was a nice person…who just happened to be a girl.

Sometimes luck is better than smarts.

Warren and Goober nearly killed everybody in town when their misfired cannon shot led to the arrest of some crooks.

A warm welcome catches a chill after three days.

Gomer was invited to stay with Andy, Opie, and Aunt Bee, but he was more "welcome" on the first day than he was on the fourth.

Cut the other guy a little slack.

Andy enforced the spirit of the law, but often not the letter of it. He left the tire chalking and the jaywalker patrolling to Barney.

To a child, swapping a penny that was run over by a train for a horse hair sounds like a good deal…who knows? Maybe it is.

Opie's swaps often seemed silly to Andy, but sometimes grown-ups need to look through a kid's eye to make sense of things.

When you start to think a lot of yourself, take a look through somebody else's eyes.

Andy convinced himself that Ellie was out to catch him as her husband. He was embarrassed to find that he was more impressed with himself than she was.

Argue only if the juice is worth the squeeze.

Andy settled a feud between two mountain families who had fought for years. When all was said and done, neither family even knew what they were fighting for in the first place!

Treat gifts from the heart with extra care.

Otis's painting wasn't much good, but it was sincere, and the Taylors hung it proudly in the living room.

You are whatever you convince
yourself you are. Faith is
90 percent of what's real.

Ernest T. Bass went back to school to get a diploma and to win the heart of the fair "Romeena." It worked. Ernest T. wasn't a lick smarter; he just believed he was—and so did "Romeena."

When asked to keep a secret, think of who could be hurt by your not telling.

Opie tried to respect the wishes of a friend, but he forgot about the pain of his pal's parents who feared that their boy was in danger.

Forget grudges…they waste time and energy.

Twenty years after graduation from Mayberry Union High, Barney couldn't forgive Jack Egbert for blackballing him from the Philomethian Literary Society—and where did it get him?

Unknown does not mean evil.

The citizens made a visitor from New York City feel unwelcome until they learned that he had been a part of Mayberry for years…in his mind.

Be kind to strangers—your best friend was a stranger once.

When Opie met Aunt Bee for the first time, he wasn't too sure about her. His faith in her was soon rewarded with more love than he could have dreamed of.

If you're discouraged, count on a true friend.

Andy tried to restore Barney's sinking confidence by arranging social and "deputy" events. There turned out to be nothing wrong with Ol' Barn that a little attention from Hilda May and some top-flight police work couldn't fix.

Barney: We're [accepted] in [the Esquire Club], ain't we?

Andy: Well, no. Fact is, they was about to accept one of us . . .

Barney: One of us. You must be kiddin'. I'd like to punch 'em all right in the nose.

Andy: Now, Barney, no use to get upset. They got the right to pick who they want, you know . . .

Barney: Imagine that. Imagine that! Turning down a nice guy like you! Who do they think they are anyway? Well they couldn't find a nicer guy than you in the whole world to be in their old club. Well, I'll show 'em.

Andy: What are you doin'?

Barney: I'll tell you what I'm doin'. If you ain't good enough for them, neither am I. I'm sending in my resignation!

From: "The Clubmen"
Original Air Date: December 11, 1961

New friends are like new shoes— they both take some time to get used to.

Newcomer druggist Ellie became friends with cantankerous Emma Watson only after they had a few less-than-friendly meetings.

Learn from the simple acts of children.

Andy learned a lesson when Opie ignored a public show of charity in favor of a true, private act of kindness.

Never burn bridges.

Jim Lindsey, Mayberry's best guitar picker, got too big for his britches and nearly blew his chance to make it in the music biz. If folks from Mayberry hadn't helped him, he'd never have made it with Bobby Fleet and His Band with the Beat.

Andy: Can you, uh, can you stay in Mayberry awhile?

Sharon de Spain: Oh, I'd love to Andy; I can't.

Andy: Why not? Mayberry's nice this time of year. . .

Sharon: I know. I enjoyed growing up here.

Andy: Oh, it's a mighty nice place. A lot of friends.

Sharon: I know. But you can't live up to your potential here. In a big city you have room to grow. To expand. You live a different kind of life.

Andy: How can life be that much different, if you're happy? That's the main thing, ain't it? That's the goal that every individual as a person is shooting for. It's kind of the prize of the game. To be happy.

From: "Class Reunion"
Original Air Date: February 4, 1963

Try to be happy. Happiness is life's great prize.

Ben, the town Scrooge, tried to ruin Christmas for a Mayberry family, but his plans failed when the spirit of Christmas touched even him.

Don't expect more from others than you are willing to give.

Barney gave Mayberry his best, and that was usually more than enough to satisfy his fellow citizens.

It may look easy to fill someone else's shoes. The looking is easy; the doing isn't.

When Andy went out of town, Barney filled his shoes for a day—and nearly destroyed the town.

Make sure you understand the
views of others before you try to
convince them that yours is right.

*The town fathers scoffed at Ellie's candidacy for
city council; they claimed that she was too inex-
perienced, too young, and...a woman.*

Words can be consoling, infor-mative or destructive—use them wisely.

A suave crook intrigued everyone but Andy, who knew how to look through words.

There are two ways to have the tallest building in town: tear others down or build yours higher.

Shopkeeper Ben Weaver was worried that Malcolm, the peddler, was invading his "turf," so he tried to drive Malcolm out of business— until Ben saw that there was room for him ...in Ben's own store.

Don't be a knucklehead. Just because somebody says it, doesn't mean it's true.

Opie took bad advice from Trey Bowden, a new kid in Mayberry, and soon regretted it.

Fly the flag; some of us have short memories.

Barney's patriotism shone through when he donated his historic motorcycle to the town in memory of Mayberry's World War II veterans.

Everyone should know the words to "Amazing Grace."

Reverend Hobart Tucker encouraged churchgoers to slow down and drink in the Lord's goodness.

Amazing grace, how sweet the sound
That saved a wretch like me!
I once was lost, but now am found;
Was blind, but now I see.

'Twas grace that taught my heart to fear,
And grace my fears relieved;
How precious did that grace appear
The hour I first believed!

Through many dangers, toils, and snares
I have already come.
'Tis grace hath brought me safe thus far
And grace will lead me home.

Trust strangers—but keep an eye on them for awhile.

The big-city film crew tried to rob the bank after flimflamming the townsfolk with their claim that they'd make Mayberry "Hollywood South."

Give things away anonymously. If you make recognition your reward for giving, you're getting paid for it.

Andy learned a lesson about charity from Opie, who innocently and purely showed the spirit of generosity.

Don't put too much pressure on your kids; don't expect them to do things that you couldn't.

Andy tried not to be disappointed in Opie's lack of athletic ability—and was reminded that there are many ways to be a champion in life.

Deal with unpleasant things now ...waiting generally makes them worse.

Andy, Opie, and Barney found that the best way to handle Aunt Bee's "kerosene cucumbers" was to eat them.

To be a real hero, accept the blame as easily as the credit.

Barney got into trouble when he wouldn't admit to Gomer that he made an illegal U-turn.

You can't say "thank you" too much.

Every day Barney thanked Andy, who believed in him enough to make him Deputy Fife.

If things are all messed up, jump in—you may just do some good.

When Barney and Thelma's courtship hit rock bottom, Andy stepped in to help, and he got things back to normal.

Write a note to someone every day.

Let folks know how you feel. A simple thank-you note once got the town choir into a state competition.

Better to be surprised than dis-appointed.

Howard was overconfident about his membership at the lodge and was almost sorely disappointed.

Life is not as difficult as we make it.

The people of Mayberry kept it simple and they enjoyed life.

Don't take yourself too seriously.

Andy's strengths compensated for Barney's weaknesses, and vice versa.

Mr. Tucker: Outrageous. Sheer idiocy. I can't believe this is happening to me. A public utility being tied up like this. You people are living in another world.

Andy: Now easy, Mr. Tucker.

Mr. Tucker: This is the twentieth century. Don't you realize that? The whole world is living in a desperate space age. Men are orbiting the earth. International television has been developed. And here, the whole town is standing still because two old women's feet fall asleep.

Barney: I wonder what causes that?

From: "Man in a Hurry"
Original Air Date: January 14, 1963

Think.

Right, Barney?

Be kind and generous.

Be like Mayberry.

Trees don't grow to the sky; quit while you're ahead.

Barney should have popped the question to Thelma Lou years ago.

Most of life's important lessons aren't fun to learn.

Opie learned this early and often—with wonderful results.

Don't treat success like a stranger.

Barney had a swelled head after he accidentally collared a crook. He changed his tune when the bad guy escaped and came gunning for him.

You can't do everything... choose carefully.

Goober couldn't fix a friend's car and answer the courthouse phone at the same time, like he promised Andy. When he brought the car into the courthouse, he couldn't do either.

Be kind. Do your best.
Be satisfied.

Aunt Bee spent her life being a model of compassion, generosity and contentment.

Friends make mistakes…true
friends forgive.

Otis caused quite a stir by filing a lawsuit against the county—but his friends, Andy and Barney, forgave him when they found that his heart wasn't really in it.

Shoot for the stars, but understand you might have to be satisfied hitting the clouds.

Aunt Bee had the desire to be Lady Mayberry but was a little short on talent. She realized that her greatest talent was taking care of her boys, Opie and Andy.

Today is the only day we have to do good. Yesterday's gone; tomorrow's not a sure thing.

Opie and Barney tried to look into the future with gypsy fortune-telling cards—and got nowhere but in trouble.

Don't do business with friends; you might lose both.

Barney nearly ruined his friendship with Andy over the real-estate business.

Don't call attention to yourself.

Jeff Pruitt was a nice enough guy, but you always knew where he was.

People can only change from the inside—you can't force it.

Old Otis was still Otis, even after Barney used his modern psychological techniques to try to change him.

In love, two's company... everybody else, get lost.

Goober never figured out for himself that "both of us" is a lot different than "all of us." He finally learned this rule when he and Lydia were stepping out.

The meaning of "friend" changes from one person to another.

Helen wanted Opie to be her pal, but Opie had a crush on Helen. They got it worked out, but it took some doin'.

Ninety percent of the things we fret over never happen anyway.

Fred Bishop threatened Barney after the deputy caught him littering. Then, Barney nearly got sick with worry that he'd run into him again. Of course, nothing ever came of it.

Youth is a way of thinking. There are some eighty-year-old "children."

Old Jud could hold his own with men half his age...he was a spry eighty.

Keep an eye on your loved ones.

Many's the night that Andy skipped his lodge meeting and stayed home to watch TV with Aunt Bee...he knew she got lonely sometimes.

Do what is right.

The Andy Griffith Show *in four words.*